The Secret Diary of Mug Cake Fantasies

Enjoy the pleasure of Mug cake recipes in a healthy way

Bobby Flatt

INTRODUCTION

Apart from its lovey dovey look and creamy texture, mug cakes are among favorites as they make the dishes and spoons least dirty & get ready in matter of minutes. Is there even single day when one cannot imagine having a mug cake? Not for me for sure!! Also I feel terribly lazy after just eating the yummy dinner stuffs, and then it takes lots of effort to pull myself to involve in hard work of making cookies or brownies in batches. One of the reasons for having a soft corner for mug cake!!

Craving for the decent sized guilt free dessert after dinner? Who else can serve your customized dessert need than mug cake; it saves you from the lengthy hours long preparation process and its right amount of single size lets you get tempted for only few seconds.

This special edition of mug cake recipe cookbook encrypts lovely & healthy fusion preparations like Blueberry Booster Cake, Cinnamon Guilt-free Swirl, Tangy Lemony Protein Cake, Protein Rich Cherry Tart Cake, Paleo Dream Mug Cake, Avocado Guilt-free Avenue, Furious Funfetti with Desirable Vanilla, and others to shift you permanently over the mug cake as a dessert replacement.

It is like become my regular habit to have something sweet post dinner and of course I don't wish to stuff up so many calories every day on dessert; so I used to have little piece of chocolate or something very tiny and sweet, before the mug cake replaced it. Be ready to be thrilled with beautiful mug cakes that will win your heart with its healthy ingredients and jaw dropping attractive looks!!

TABLE OF CONTENTS

PROTEIN BOOSTED MUG CAKE FANTACIES

PROTEIN BOOSTER BERRY CAKE

This Berry mug cake does not make any compromise on either protein supplement or rich flavor. The combination of blackberries with almond mixture makes it real treat to have!!

Prep Time: 4 min

Serving Size: 1 mug cake

INGREDIENTS:

- Blackberries – 8 To 10 Pieces
- Protein Powder, Vanilla - 1/4 Cup
- Coconut Oil - 2 Tsp.
- Vanilla or Plain Yogurt - 1 Tbs.
- Maple Syrup - 1 Tsp.
- Baking Powder - 1 Tsp.
- Vanilla Extract - 1 Tsp.
- Egg White - 3 Tbs.
- Almond Extract - 1 Tsp.

DIRECTIONS:

1. In the beginning of the cake making process; take the mug and mix in yogurt, extracts, coconut oil, and egg white. Mix them quite nicely.
2. Next, take your mixing bowl (medium or large). Mix in maple syrup and berries. Mix them quite nicely.
3. In the mixture prepared in the mug; mix both protein and baking powder. Lastly add berries to it and mix well.
4. Put it to bake inside microwave for the next 2-3 minutes. Take out to enjoy all delicacies captured inside the mug!!

PROTEIN CAKE WITH JUICY STRAWBERRIES

Are you another strawberry cake fan? Well, I am certainly the fan for sure. This protein booster is the true body builder in disguise; this mug cakes is absolutely shame-free. Starting from strawberry sprinkled moist cake to yogurt oozing from its top, every part of the mug cake involves clean ingredients to infuse your body with muscle builder protein making it a must to have post workout mug cake.

Prep Time: 4 min

Serving Size: 1 mug cake

INGREDIENTS:

To make the Cake:

- Coconut Flour – 1 ½ tbs.
- Baking Powder - ½ tsp.
- Protein Powder, Vanilla Casein - 1 Scoop
- Apple Sauce, Unsweetened - 1 tbs.
- Strawberry, - 1 piece, cubed
- Almond Milk, Unsweetened - ¼ Cup + 1 tbs.
- Egg - 1
- Vanilla Extract - ½ tsp.
- Stevia as required

To prepare the Topping:

- Greek Yogurt - 2 tbs.
- Stevia, to taste
- Almond Milk, Unsweetened - ½ tbs.
- Strawberries - 2-3 pieces, cubed
- Vanilla Extract - ⅛ tsp.
- Coconut, chopped - ½ tbs. unsweetened

DIRECTIONS:

1. In the beginning of the cake making process; take the mug and mix in all cake ingredients in it. First mix in dry ingredients and then wet ones. Mix them quite nicely.
2. Then after, add strawberries (cubed); it will make batter little more thick.
3. Put it to bake inside microwave for the next 3 minutes. In between, start preparing the topping.
4. Take your mixing bowl (medium or large). Mix in almond milk, yogurt, stevia, and vanilla extract. Mix them quite nicely. Let it chill in the refrigerator till cake gets ready.
5. Add prepared topping over the cake, do the garnishing with strawberries and enjoy all its delicacies captured inside the mug!!

BLUEBERRY BOOSTER CAKE

Are you in the mood to blast massive amount of protein into your blood stream? And who can resist the juicy taste of blueberries? Addition of coconut cream on the top gives it the lovely finish!!

Prep Time: 10 min

Serving Size: 1 mug cake

INGREDIENTS:

- Protein Powder, Vanilla - 1 Scoop
- Quick Oats - 2 tbs.
- Coconut Flour - 1 tbs.
- Baking Powder - 1 1/2 tsp.
- Almond Milk, Vanilla - 1/2 Cup
- Stevia - 3 Packs
- Egg Whites - 1/2 Cup
- Blueberries - 1/4 Cup

Coconut Cream:
- Coconut flour - 1 tbs.
- Water – 1 to 3 tbs.
- Stevia - 2 packs

DIRECTIONS:

1. In the beginning of the cake making process; take the mug and mix in all ingredients mentioned above. Mix them quite nicely.
2. Put it to bake inside microwave for the next 6-7 minutes.
3. Meanwhile, make the coconut cream by mixing all its ingredients. When cake gets ready, pour the cream on top of it. Enjoy the pleasure of prepared mug cake!!

VANILLA MORNING WITH WHOLE-GRAIN CAKE

Being a protein rich mug cake, the cake recipe is the perfect alternative for grainoholics out there. The lightened up version of cake includes flax seed meal, and wheat bran to supply with essential nutrients along with heavenly taste!!

Prep Time:	4 min
Serving Size:	1 mug cake

INGREDIENTS:

- Skim Milk - 4 tbs.
- Wheat Bran - 3 tbs.
- Flax Seed Meal, Ground - 4 tbs.
- Oats - 2 tbs.
- Protein Powder, Vanilla - 1 Scoop
- Egg White - 1 piece
- Baking Powder - 1/4 tsp.
- Vanilla Extract - 1 tsp.
- Cinnamon, Ground - 1/4 tsp.

DIRECTIONS:

1. In the beginning of the cake making process; take the mug and mix in all ingredients mentioned above. Mix them quite nicely.
2. Put it to bake inside microwave for the next 2-3 minutes. Take out and let it cool down. Enjoy the pleasure of prepared mug cake!!

Pumpkin Chocolate Booster Cake

Pumpkin Chocolate Booster Cake is almost Paleo cake and packs with lots of good stuff. The tasty cake made me feel sad with the realization of having the last bite of it. I hate that feeling!! ☺ The taste of chocolate and pumpkin made me feel like having it non-stop!!

Prep Time: 4 min

Serving Size: 1 mug cake

INGREDIENTS:

- Vanilla protein powder - 1 scoop
- Few chocolate chips
- Pureed pumpkin - 1/4 cup
- Egg whites - 2 pieces
- Pumpkin spice - 1 tsp.
- Almond flour - 1 tbs.
- Vanilla extract - 1 tsp.
- Stevia - 2 packets
- Baking powder - 1/2 tsp.
- Cooking spray

DIRECTIONS:

1. In the beginning of the cake making process; take the mug and grease it nicely.
2. Then after, mix in all the ingredients. Mix them quite nicely to avoid any lumps.
3. Put it to bake inside microwave for the next 2-3 minutes. Take out to enjoy all delicacies captured inside the mug!!
4. Pour the select toppings on top of the mug.
5. For Toppings: You have many options like chocolate shavings, coconut shavings, whipped cream, chocolate sauce, ice cream, maple syrup, jams, or any of your preferred one!

TANGY LEMONY PROTEIN CAKE

Craving for the iced lemon tea to end the desire for having something tangy? Then, this mug recipe is the healthy alternative by being low in sugar content and caloric value. Must have for lemon freaks!!

Prep Time: 2 min

Serving Size: 1 mug cake

INGREDIENTS:

- Oat flour - 3 tbs.
- Baking powder - 1/2 tsp.
- Stevia packs as required
- Vanilla protein powder - 1 tbs.
- Lemon juice - 1 tbs.
- Salt pinch
- Plain yogurt - 3 tbs.
- Lemon zest -1 tsp.
- Egg white – 1

DIRECTIONS:

1. In the beginning of the cake making process; take the mug and prepare it by using cooking spray.
2. Then after, mix in all the ingredients. First mix in dry ingredients and then wet ones. Mix them quite nicely to avoid any lumps.
3. Put it to bake inside microwave for the next 2 minutes or till nicely settles down. Take out to enjoy all delicacies captured inside the mug!!

DIVA VANILLA DANCE WITH CARAMEL PROTEIN

It's time to try out this dancing diva cake with amazing caramel flavor. I made this cake when I craved strongly for the dessert by adding some of my favorite ingredients like stevia and caramel extract; guess what it clicked just right!!

Prep Time: 5 min

Serving Size: 1 mug cake

INGREDIENTS:

- Coconut flour - 3 tbs.
- Stevia - 2 packs
- Plain yogurt - 3 tbs.
- Baking powder - 1/4 tsp.
- Caramel extract - 1 tsp.
- Protein powder, vanilla milkshake - 1/2 scoop
- Water - 4 tbs.

DIRECTIONS:

1. In the start of making the cake; take the mug and prepare it by using cooking spray.
2. Then after, mix in all the ingredients. First mix in dry ingredients and then wet ones. Mix them quite nicely to avoid any lumps.
3. Put it to bake inside microwave for the next 2 minutes or till nicely settles down. Take out to enjoy all delicacies captured inside the mug!!
4. Top the mug with almond butter (melted). Feel free to experiment with your own combinations!!

PROTEIN BOOSTER CARROT CAKE

I got the idea of adding my all-time favorite veggie "Carrot" in the mug cake after hearing about mug cakes from all around. As always, the addition of carrot did not disappoint me. If you are one of the person who wants to enjoy the carrots cake, but without adding much of butter or oil in making it; this cake is just the right one for you!!

Prep Time: 5 min

Serving Size: 1 mug cake

INGREDIENTS:

- Egg whites - 2
- Grated carrot - 1/4 cup
- Quick oats - 1/4 cup
- Protein powder, vanilla - 1/2 tbs.
- Nutmeg - 1/8 tsp.
- Cinnamon - 1/4 tsp.
- Vanilla extract - 1/4 tsp.
- Vanilla almond milk, unsweetened - 1 tbs.
- Baking powder - 1/4 tsp.
- Splenda - 1 packet

For Frosting:
- Greek yogurt, plain - 2 tbs.
- Vanilla almond milk, unsweetened - 1 tsp.
- Protein powder, vanilla - 1 tsp.
- Splenda - 1 packet

DIRECTIONS:

1. At first, take your mixing bowl (medium or large). Mix in all the dry ingredients.
2. Then mix in egg white, carrot, vanilla extract, and milk to it. Mix them quite nicely.
3. Then after, pour in prepared bowl mixture.
4. Put it inside microwave for the next 2-3 minutes or for more time till nicely settles down. Take out and let it gradually cool down.
5. Make the frosting by nicely mixing up all the ingredients for it. Place the frosting on top of the prepared cake to make it more unresisting to eat.
6. Lastly add finely chopped carrots over the frosting. Enjoy your mug cake!!

CHOCOLATY CAKE RETREAT WITH PROTEIN AND MINT

I am one of the chocolate addicts who can't stop thinking about it every time I have the dessert. Then I found this version, which does not only satisfy my sweet tooth, but also prevent me from having any micro guilt.

This protein booster version with addition of chocolate is incredibly simple to make. The cake also packs less than 150 calories to motivate the healthy bug residing inside you. The scent of mint in the mug cake is so exhilarating and thrilling!!

Image Credit: Flickr user Somebody 3lse, <https://www.flickr.com/photos/s0mebody3lse/3302974022/sizes/l>

Prep Time: 5 min

Serving Size: 1 mug cake

INGREDIENTS:

- Chocolate Protein - 1 scoop
- Stevia - 1 tbs.
- Cocoa powder - 1 tbs.
- Mint extract - 1/8 tsp.
- Baking powder - 1/4 tsp.
- Coconut milk, unsweetened - 6 tbs.

DIRECTIONS:

1. At first, take your mixing bowl (medium or large). Mix in all the ingredients. Mix them quite nicely.
2. Prepare the mug by evenly spraying cooking spray. Alternatively you can use coconut oil to coat in nicely.
3. Then after, pour in prepared bowl mixture in the sprayed mug.
4. Let the mug mixture microwave for the next 2-3 minutes or for more time till nicely settles down. Take out and let it gradually cool down.
5. Top the mug cake with chocolate syrup (Sugar-free) and mint leaves. Enjoy!!

GUILT FREE MUG CAKES FANTASIES

CINNAMON GUILT-FREE SWIRL

After experimenting so much on mug cakes, I just cannot stop myself from trying out it with cinnamon. It's hard to experiment and then discover recipes that take only few minutes to get into shape as I am not the waiting lover, when it comes to food. This cake not only prepares in few minutes, it also has the amazing moist texture. Have it to enjoy every bit of its cinnamon roll on top!!

Prep Time: 5 min

Serving Size: 1 mug cake

INGREDIENTS:

- Applesauce - 2 tbs.
- Buttermilk - 1 tbs.
- Vegetable oil - 1 tbs.
- Flour, all-purpose - 1/4 cup + 1 tbs.
- Vanilla extract - 1/4 tsp.
- Brown sugar - 2 1/2 tbs.
- Nutmeg, Ground - 1 dash (optional)
- Cinnamon, Ground - 3/4 tsp.
- Baking powder - 1/4 tsp.
- Salt - 1/8 tsp. (scant)

To make Cream Cheese Icing:
- Powdered sugar - 2 tbs.
- Cream cheese, softened - 1 tbs.
- Milk - 1 tsp.

DIRECTIONS:

To make Icing:
1. At first, take your mixing bowl (medium or large). Mix in all icing ingredients. Mix them quite nicely with a fork.

To make mug cake:
1. In the beginning of the cake making process; take the mug and mix in all mentioned ingredients. Mix them quite nicely to avoid any lumps.
2. Let the mug mixture microwave for the next 1-2 minutes or for more time till gets done as desired. Take out and let it gradually cool down.
3. Top it with prepared crème icing and then enjoy the pleasure of prepared mug cake!!

MUG CAKE MANIA WITH SWEET POTATO

This mug cake is the culprit behind shifting me from once a week cake maker to trice a week mug cake freak. I like this cake's out of the blue soft texture with the taste of yummy sweet potato. Try out this week without a fail!!

Prep Time: 10 min

Serving Size: 2 mug cake

INGREDIENTS:

- Egg substitute - 1 tbs.
- Mashed sweet potatoes, cooked - 1/4 cup
- Water - 1/4 cup
- Soy or almond milk - 2 tbs.
- Brown sugar - 1/4 cup
- Vanilla extract - 1/4 tsp.
- Flour, self-rising - 7 tbs.
- Cinnamon - 1/2 tsp. Ground
- Grated nutmeg - 1/2 tsp.
- Toasted walnuts - 3 tbs. chopped (optional)
- Ginger - 1/2 tsp. Ground
- Salt as required

DIRECTIONS:

1. In the beginning of the cake making process; take the mug and mix in water and egg substitute. Mix them quite nicely and set the bowl aside.
2. Then after, mix in soy milk, sweet potato, sugar, salt, spices, flour and vanilla. Beat to make it real smooth. Lastly add in nuts.
3. Take two separate mugs and add equal amount of batter in them.
4. Let the mug mixture microwave for the next 2 to 2 ½ minutes or for more time till gets done as desired. Take out and let it gradually cool down. Repeat the same for other mug!!

HAZELNUT HURRICANE WITH GUILT-FREE CHOCOLATE

Who can resist himself from exploring hazelnut reach cake that gets ready in less than 5 minutes? Not to forget its chocolaty taste to make it unforgettable experience!!

Image Credit: Flickr user Mr. Michael Phams,
<https://www.flickr.com/photos/michaelphams/3285263773/sizes/o/>

Prep Time: 5 min

Serving Size: 1 mug cake

INGREDIENTS:

- Flour, all purpose - 3 tbs.
- Baking powder - ¼ tsp.
- Cocoa powder, unsweetened - 1 tbs.
- Butter, chocolate hazelnut - 1½ tbs.
- Egg - 1
- Sugar - 1 tbs.
- Unsweetened applesauce - 1 tbs.
- Milk - 3 tbs.
- Vegetable oil - 1½ tbs.

DIRECTIONS:

1. At first, prepare the mug by evenly spraying cooking spray. Alternatively you can use coconut oil to coat in nicely.
2. In the mug, mix in all the ingredients by using a fork.
3. Let the mug mixture microwave for the next about 3 minutes or for more time till gets done as desired. Take out and let it gradually cool down.
4. You can top the cake with whipped cream, if desired. Enjoy all delicacies captured inside the mug!!

GERMAN GOOFY CAKE

If you are looking for the replacement over your butter-filled pastries, then you won't need to waste any more time. German goofy cake creates perfect combination of coconut oil, whole-wheat flour, and protein powder (chocolate flavor) by infusing only 250 calories in one serving!! How guilt-free any cake can be than that?

Image Credit: Flickr user ThePinkPeppercorn,
<https://www.flickr.com/photos/gail_thepinkpeppercorn/5587046523/sizes/l>

Prep Time: 3 min

Serving Size: 1 mug cake

INGREDIENTS:

- Egg white - 1
- Almond milk, unsweetened - 4 tbs.
- Coconut oil - 1 tsp.
- Whole-wheat flour - 2 tbs.
- Cocoa powder - 1.5 tbs.
- Chocolate protein powder - 1 tbs.
- Baking powder - 1/8 tsp.
- Sugar, coconut palm - 1 tbs.
- Baking soda - 1/8 tsp.

DIRECTIONS:

1. In the beginning of the cake making process; take the mixing bowl and mix in all dry ingredients first. Then add in all wet ones. Mix them quite nicely to avoid any lumps.
2. Prepare the mug by evenly spraying cooking spray. Alternatively you can use coconut oil to coat in nicely.
3. Then after, pour in prepared bowl mixture in the sprayed mug.
4. Let the mug mixture microwave for the just above 1 minute minutes or for more time till gets done as desired.
5. Take out and enjoy the lovely mug cake!!

CREAMY CAKE WITH BERRY FIREWORKS

Chocolate chips (vegan), coconut flakes, ground almonds, and almond milk makes up lovely combination to form the desired cake. Enjoy this little naughty gluten free, refined sugar-free, and also soy free mug cake!!

Prep Time: 5 min

Serving Size: 1 mug cake

INGREDIENTS:

Cake:
- Vegan chocolate chips - 1/4 cup
- Coconut flakes - 2 tbs.
- Ground almonds - 2 tbs.
- Almond milk - 1 tsp.
- Rum extract (optional)

Cream:
- Coconut milk yogurt – 2 to 3 tbs.
- Raw sugar, ground or sweetener of choice - 1 tsp.
- Cinnamon – pinch full

Topping:
- Sliced strawberries
- Blueberries or Blackberries

DIRECTIONS:

1. In the bowl, mix in chocolate and put it for microwave till melts in nicely. Then after, add liquor extract (optional), almond milk, coconut flakes, ground almonds and spices of choice in the melted chocolate bowl. Mix smoothly.
2. Slice up the fruits in advance and let them chilled in the refrigerator.
3. To make the cream; take the bowl, mix in sugar, mix yogurt, and pinch full of cinnamon. Mix nicely and set aside.
4. Prepare the mug by evenly spraying cooking spray. Alternatively you can use coconut oil to coat in nicely.
5. Then after, pour in prepared chocolate mixture in the sprayed mug.

6. Let the mug mixture microwave for the next 2-3 minutes or for more time till gets done as desired. Take out and let it gradually cool down.

7. Spread nicely the prepared cream over the mug and then top it with sliced fruits. Again put in in the refrigerator to chill down for at least 30 minutes. Take out and enjoy!!

OUTSTANDING OATMEAL CAKE

Pecans and oats combine to form a delicious concoction which is being made indulgent and rich by putting a Nutella dollop in its center. A little more of baking powder and letting our eggs from the recipe is making it all fluffy and light. If Nutella is not something that you are into, then you can replace it with cooked fruit and butter.

Prep Time: 5 min

Serving Size: 1 mug cake

INGREDIENTS:

- Milk - 3 tbs.
- Sugar - 1 tbs.
- Olive oil - 1 tbs.
- Flour - 3 tbs.
- Pecans, finely chopped - 1 tbs.
- Rolled oats - 1 1/2 tbs.
- Baking powder - 1/4 tsp.
- Chocolate-hazelnut spread (Nutella) - 1 tbs.
- Cinnamon - 1/4 tsp. (optional)
- Salt - 1/8 tsp.
- Pinch nutmeg, optional

DIRECTIONS:

1. In the beginning of the cake making process; take the mug and mix in olive oil, milk and sugar. Whip it nicely.
2. Then add in flour and again whisk it. Now mix in cinnamon, pecans, oats, salt, baking powder, and nutmeg. Mix them quite nicely to avoid any lumps.
3. On top of the mug mixture, add one spoon of Nutella spread.
4. Let the mug mixture microwave for the about 30-60 seconds or for more time till gets done as desired. Keep microwave on High temperature setting.
5. Take out and let it gradually cool down as the top portion of the cake will be hot for some time.
6. You can decorate with Nutella spread, if desired. Enjoy the naughty Nutella cake!!

PALEO DREAM MUG CAKE

Paleo dream mug cake gets ready in the blink of the time. Almond flour and coconut makes up for the base, while addition of eggs in it holds all of the ingredients together. Mix in vanilla extract and maple syrup for the required sweetness. The end burst of chocolate chips makes up for the perfect ending!!

Image Credit: Flickr user Cherryred's Beardy,
<https://www.flickr.com/photos/ubercherryred/4370909617/sizes/l>

Prep Time: 2 min

Serving Size: 1 mug cake

INGREDIENTS:

- Egg - 1 large
- Almond flour - 1 tbs.
- Coconut flour - 1 tbs.
- Chocolate chips - 2 tbs.
- Vanilla - 1 tbs.
- Maple syrup - 2 tbs.

DIRECTIONS:

1. In the beginning of the cake making process; take the mug and whisk one egg in it. Beat it nicely.
2. Now add in all remaining ingredients. Mix them quite nicely to avoid any lumps.
3. Let the mug mixture microwave for the next 1 1/2 minutes or for more time till gets done as desired. Take out and let it gradually cool down.
4. Then enjoy all delicacies captured inside the mug!!

ALMOND MUG MAGIC WITH GUILT-FREE BANANA

Almond mug magic requires only 1/3rd cup banana to add the desired sweetness in the mug cake. Almond flour and coconut flour provides the nutritious dose of protein and fiber. What else one can expect from the dessert which offers less than 100 calories and more than 5 grams of protein?

Prep Time: 5 min

Serving Size: 4 mug cake

INGREDIENTS:

- Butter - 2 tbs.
- Almond flour - 1/3 cup
- Ripe banana, mashed - 1/3 cup
- Almond butter - 1 tbs.
- Baking powder - 1/2 tsp.
- Egg - 1
- Vanilla extract -1/2 tsp.
- Coconut flour - 1 tbs.
- Salt – pinch full

DIRECTIONS:

1. At first, melt the butter smoothly. Then after, take the mixing salad bowl and mix all the ingredients including melted butter. Continue mixing till mixes well with each other.
2. Now take the 4 mugs and pour the mixture equally into them.
3. Let the mug mixture microwave for the about 90 seconds minutes or for more time till gets done as desired. Take out and let it gradually cool down. Repeat the same with other 3 mugs.
4. You can top the cake with banana slice or whipped cream. Enjoy the pleasure of warm mug cake!!

AVOCADO GUILT-FREE AVENUE

Avocado Avenue contains no use of any artificial colors, it is avocado written all over it. Avocado mug cake do includes some of the sugar content, but you can escape it by using Stevia or by cutting down on sweetener. Experiment both the version and choose your favorite!!

Prep Time: 5 min

Serving Size: 1 mug cake

INGREDIENTS:

- Flour - 4 tbs.
- Baking powder - 1/4 tsp.
- Sugar - 4 1/2 tbs.
- Milk, Fat-free - 5 tbs.
- Mashed avocado - 3 tbs.

DIRECTIONS:

1. In the beginning of the cake making process; take the mug and mix in all cake ingredients. Mix them quite nicely to avoid any lumps.
2. Let the mug mixture microwave for the next 2 or 2 1/2 minutes or till top most portion of the cake becomes completely dry. Take out and let it gradually cool down.
3. Enjoy the cake!! You can put some whipped cream on top, if desired.

COCONUTY & CHOCOLATY CUTIE CAKE

Coconuty & Chocolaty Cutie Cake is the fastest way to make high-protein, low-carb, and high-fiber mug cake. The richness of its texture is sponsored by surprising addition of vanilla bean seeds. Ones cooked nicely, dress the mug cake with peanut butter to take its beauty the next level!!

Prep Time: 5 min

Serving Size: 1 mug cake

INGREDIENTS:

- Coconut flour - 1 tbs.
- Baking soda - 1/4 tsp.
- Cocoa - 1 tbs.
- Salt as required
- Coconut or almond milk - 3 tbs.
- Honey - 1 tbs.
- Egg - 1
- Vanilla - 1/2 pod, seeds discarded
- Chocolate chips for sprinkling (optional)

DIRECTIONS:

1. In the beginning of the cake making process; take the mug and mix in all dry ingredients first. Then after, it's time for wet ingredients to add. Mix both ingredients quite nicely to avoid any lumps.
2. Let the mug mixture microwave for the next 1 1/2 minutes or for more time till gets done as desired. Take out and let it gradually cool down.
3. Lastly you can add up cashew cream Nuts, ice cream, chocolate chips, or peanut butter on top of prepared cake. All are lovely choices to go with!!

TAHINI BUCKWHEAT CAKE DAY-OUT

Tahini is a special ingredient also being known as sesame butter, which is the powerhouse of calcium. Not just it's the treat for taste buds, but also for the bones. Buckwheat with the lovely taste of tahini is the cutest heavenly combination to experience. At last, the sweetness of dates put the mug cake in the driver seat to give you the thrilling cake treat!!

Image Credit: Flickr user Carol and Co, <https://www.flickr.com/photos/carolandco/15731028590/sizes/l>

Prep Time: 5 min

Serving Size: 1 mug cake

INGREDIENTS:

- Buckwheat flour - 2 tbs.
- Coconut oil - 1 tsp. (melted)
- Oats - 2 tbs. (fine)
- Tahini - 1 tsp.
- Chia seeds - 1 tsp.
- Tiger nuts - 1 tsp. (optional)
- Baking soda - ¼ tsp.
- Cinnamon, ginger and salt as required
- Dates – 1 to 2 (Optional)
- Almonds - 1 handful (chopped)
- Rice milk as required

DIRECTIONS:

1. In the beginning of the cake making process; take the mug and mix in first all dry ingredients. Spare some almonds to decorate on the cake later. Mix them quite nicely.
2. Now in the mixture of dry ingredients, pour in rice milk, and coconut oil. Stir them smoothly to mix very well to avoid any lumps.
3. Let the mixture settle down for 5 minutes. If the mixture feels to dry, then you can add in some rice milk to make it ideal to stir.
4. If you prefer your mug cake to be little sweet, then chop up one or two dates and add the dates in the mixture.
5. Now place the left over almonds over the mug mixture.
6. Let the mug mixture microwave for the next 2-3 minutes or for more time till gets done as desired. Take out and let it gradually cool down.
7. On top of it, drizzle up some tahini, if you want. Enjoy all delicacies captured inside the mug!!

PROTEIN RICH CHERRY TART CAKE

This special mug cake tastes little tangy by adding little quantity of orange zest. The lovely finishing touch comes with cherry and whipped cream on the top of it.

Prep Time: 5 min

Serving Size: 1 mug cake

INGREDIENTS:

- Peanut butter, powdered - 2 tbs.
- Milk - 3 tbs.
- Protein powder, vanilla whey - 1 tbs.
- Almond butter, unsweetened - 1 tbs.
- Dash of orange zest, grated
- Dash of salt
- Honey - 2 tsp.
- Cherries – 5 pieces, frozen tart
- Whipped cream for garnishing

DIRECTIONS:

1. In the beginning of the cake making process; take the mixing bowl (medium or large) and mix in peanut butter, milk, protein powder, honey, salt, and almond butter. Mix them quite nicely to avoid any lumps.
2. Then add up cherries gradually in the batter.
3. Prepare the mug by evenly spraying cooking spray. Alternatively you can use coconut oil to coat in nicely.
4. Then after, pour in prepared bowl mixture in the sprayed mug.
5. Let the mug mixture microwave for the next 2-3 minutes or for more time till gets done as desired. Take out and let it gradually cool down.
6. You can top it with either yogurt, whipped cream, or your favorite ice-crème. Enjoy your self-made cake!!

PEANUT BUTTER CAKE WITH PEANUT PURE FROSTING

This all peanut recipe adds one more secret peanut ingredient in the form of peanut flour. The fiber rich mug cake also contains loads of proteins and little of fat to keep you all curvy even after having it again and again.

Prep Time: 5 min

Serving Size: 1 mug cake

INGREDIENTS:

- Ground Flaxseed - 1 tbs.
- Applesauce, Unsweetened - 1/4 cup
- Almond Milk, Unsweetened - 1/3 cup
- Truvia - 4 packs
- Oat Flour - 1/4 cup
- Baking Powder - 1 tsp.
- Salt - 1/8 tsp.
- Peanut Flour - 1/4 cup
- Frosting Peanut Butter

DIRECTIONS:

1. In the beginning of the cake making process; prepare the mug by evenly spraying cooking spray. Alternatively you can use coconut oil to coat in nicely.
2. Next, take your mixing bowl (medium or large). Mix in almond milk and flax. Mix them quite nicely. Then after, add up salt, truvia, and applesauce. Again mix them.
3. Now add in peanut flour, baking powder, and oat flour. Mix well to avoid any lumps.
4. Then after, pour in prepared bowl mixture in the sprayed mug.
5. Let the mug mixture microwave for the next 6 minutes or for more time till gets done as desired. Take out and let it gradually cool down.
6. Decorate with peanut butter frosting or any of your choice of toppings. Enjoy the pleasure of prepared mug cake!!

FURIOUS FUNFETTI WITH DESIRABLE VANILLA

Furious Funfetti is one of the crazy and delicious dairy-free & egg-free mug cakes that suits every occasion. Its vibrant look feels like eating the rainbow on the dining table. Enjoy this colorful treat on the next Sunday evening!!

Prep Time: 5 min

Serving Size: 1 mug cake

INGREDIENTS:

- All-purpose flour - 1/4 cup
- Pinch of salt
- Granulated sugar - 2 tbs.
- Baking powder - 1/2 tsp.
- Pure vanilla extract - 1/2 tsp.
- Coconut or almond milk - 1/4 cup
- Sprinkles - 2 tsp.
- Coconut oil, melted - 1 1/2 tbs.

DIRECTIONS:

1. In the beginning of the cake making process; take your mixing bowl (medium or large) and mix in sugar, baking powder, flour, and salt. Mix them quite nicely to avoid any lumps.
2. Make an empty circle in the bowl center; then mix in oil, vanilla, and milk. Mix all together nicely. Lastly add in sprinkles to the batter.
3. Prepare the mug by evenly spraying cooking spray. Alternatively you can use coconut oil to coat in nicely.
4. Then after, pour in prepared bowl mixture in the sprayed mug.
5. Let the mug mixture microwave for the about 90-120 seconds or for more time till gets done as desired. Take out and let it gradually cool down.
6. On top of the cake, decorate with frozen yogurt or ice cream dollop. Then enjoy all the mug cake delicacies captured inside of it!!

DOUBLE DECKER CHOCOLATE BLAST

However the cake is of single serving, it tastes double rich by including loads of chocolate to it. Enjoy this dairy-free and gluten-free chocolate blast to make the perfect day ending!!

Prep Time: 5 min

Serving Size: 1 mug cake

INGREDIENTS:

- Almond meal - 1 tbs.
- Sugar - 2 tbs.
- Flour blend, gluten free - 1 tbs.
- Cocoa powder, unsweetened - 1¾ tbs.
- Baking soda - ⅛ tsp.
- Chocolate chips, dairy free - 1½ tbs.
- Canola oil - ½ tsp.
- Water - 3 tbs.
- Vinegar - ⅛ tsp.
- Chopped pecans - 1 tbs. (optional)
- Salt as required

DIRECTIONS:

1. In the beginning of the cake making process; take your mixing bowl (medium or large) and mix in almond meal, sugar, salt, flour blend (gluten free), baking soda, and cocoa powder. Mix them quite nicely to avoid any lumps.
2. Then after, mix in chocolate chips, vinegar, water, and oil in the bowl. Mix all of them real nice.
3. Prepare the mug by evenly spraying cooking spray. Alternatively you can use coconut oil to coat in nicely.
4. Then after, pour in prepared bowl mixture in the sprayed mug.
5. Let the mug mixture microwave for the next 75 to 90 seconds or for more time till gets done as desired. Take out and let it gradually cool down.
6. Decorate with pecans on the cake top. Enjoy!!

Buckwheat Buckle Mug with Chocolaty Banana

This mug cake is the result of my experiences with cakes; I tried it out with buckwheat flour and I got super lucky again with the end results. It feels like giving myself a little treat after successful kitchen day!! Opps, I forget to tag that it's also Vegan and dairy-free.

Prep Time:	5 min
Serving Size:	1 mug cake

INGREDIENTS:

- Buckwheat flour - 2-4 tbs.
- Banana - ½ sliced
- Cocoa powder - 1 tbs. (unsweetened)
- Rice milk - 2-4 tbs.
- Coconut oil - 1 tbs.
- Salt as required
- Cinnamon – pinch full
- Almonds - 1 handful chopped
- Baking soda - 1 pinch

DIRECTIONS:

1. In the beginning of the cake making process; take your mixing bowl (medium or large) and mix in cocoa powder, mix flour, salt, cinnamon, coconut oil, and baking soda. Mix them quite nicely to avoid any lumps.
2. Then after, mix in adequate rice milk to make the mixture of ideal consistency. Do not make it too dry to bake.
3. Prepare the mug by evenly spraying cooking spray. Alternatively you can use coconut oil to coat in nicely.
4. Then after, pour in prepared bowl mixture in the sprayed mug. On top of mug mixture, make layers of banana slices till it reaches 2/3 of mug height.
5. On top part of the mixture, sprinkle some almonds (chopped).
6. Let the mug mixture microwave for the next 2-3 minutes or for more time till gets done as desired. Take out and let it gradually cool down. Enjoy!!

Cornbread & Pumpkin Fiesta Cake

Another golden addition to your vegan, guilt-free, and yummy collection of mug cake recipes. The creamy texture and its low caloric values make it one of the most desirable cake recipes!!

Prep Time: 5 min

Serving Size: 1 mug cake

INGREDIENTS:

- Organic Cornmeal - 2 tbs.
- Baking Powder - 1/4 Tsp.
- Flour, Gluten-Free and also All-Purpose - 3 tbs.
- Baking Soda - 1/4 tsp.
- Vanilla Extract, Bourbon - 1/4 tsp.
- Cinnamon- 1/2 Tsp.
- Liquid Stevia – 8 drops
- Water - 3 tbs.
- Pumpkin Puree - 3 tbs.

DIRECTIONS:

1. In the beginning of the cake making process; take the mug and mix in all the ingredients. Mix them quite nicely to avoid any lumps.
2. Let the mug mixture microwave for the about 30-40 minutes or for more time till gets done as desired. Take out and let it gradually cool down.
3. Top it with your favorite choice among pumpkin butter, nut butter, or protein frosting. Enjoy!!

CPSIA information can be obtained at www.ICGtesting.com
Printed in the USA
LVIW01n1217301016
510908LV00003B/11

* 9 7 8 1 5 1 5 0 4 2 8 4 6 *